Tape Dispenser

Keara Kob

BookLeaf
Publishing
India | USA | UK

Presentation by *BookLeaf Publishing*

Web: www.bookleafpub.com

E-mail: info@bookleafpub.com

ISBN : 9789357448277

First edition 2021

DEDICATION

For Winry and Al

The Moment You Betrayed Me

The first time we talked,
I mean really really talked,
my father lay on his sickbed
family gathered round close
and fearful. Death pounded
eagerly on the front door.
We snuck out the back,
you and I, for a smoke.
How we dragged that
sick man in between drags.

I thought you were
a fellow carrion crow on the hunt
for a passing fancy, an amusing gall.
We lit up the town, our laughter the warbling
of hyenas feasting on a carcass.
I slunk home to mourn my own carcass.
There stood I in the oil black feathers
with my flock and handed out the
fluttering white tissues so that
they would all remember me as
the bone dry shoulder they cried on.

And when you found me
sobbing alone for myself,
once the parade had passed
and mourners filed away. I expected you
to laugh at me.
To scoff and chortle, have a riot
at my expense, the self-absorbed
heartless harpy who could not muster
a single civil word all wake.

'But no,' thought you, merciless devil,
No. Laughing at my expense would reek
too much of charity.
Instead you, dastardly villain,
you sat beside me. Brought
my head gentle to your chest
and let me cry until the
rancor had seeped
like venom
from my
veins.

Why Hannah Montana's "Hoedown Throwdown" should be the National Anthem

Crown thy good with brotherhood
O' Great America,
Have you ever had brothers?
Those weak boys
who shout into empty valleys and corridors;
since even the last emotion, anger,
was robbed of them by the haunting
shadow of failed fathers.

And a hood of them?
Let's be honest, only if they're white, right?
But really, a hood of brothers,
That's just called a mancave.

The stench of which not even
Mother's finest home brewed detergent
is able to scrub the stain of sweat away,
even after they flew the coop
to roost in some other nest.

Maybe I just don't understand?
Since sisterhood is reserved
For witches and sororities,
And tiaraing thy good just
Doesn't have the same pizzaz.
But isn't that just the point
Of the matter?

That the boom de clap of my sister's
heart beats in time with my brother's
as we stand hand in hand on the picket line,
dining on nothing but hope and brine.
Cause we'd rather starve for change,
than break our backs mining a rich man's coal.
So we each bring our brotherhoods, sisterhoods,
otherhoods, throw it all together, that's how we
roll.

Stone Eyes

Polished stone statue
reading my soul in its gaze.
Chiseled granite blinks.

Sixteen in Two-thousand and Fifteen

She lounged in the mimosa tree in the backyard,
spindly limbs and harsh angles like a marionette
draped on the branches.
It must have scared the neighbors.
The news said it was official, more Americans
weren't middle class than were.
She didn't listen to the news. She spent her time
in daydreams.
A one eyed parrot watched from the front door,
watched the woods across the street.

The news said it was official, gun deaths were as
common as traffic deaths.
It must have scared the neighbors.
She lounged in the mimosa tree in the backyard
of her middle class house.
Watched the woods across the street, she
daydreamed, of how her spindly limbs
would move if a neighbor came out of the woods
across the street with a gun and shot her.

People do things like that when they're scared.

She spent her time in daydreams. People do
things like that when they're scared.
The news said it was official, more deaths from
terrorist attacks ever since 9/11.
It must have scared the neighbors, mexican
immigrants, more of them leaving
than coming in, the news said it was official.
The mimosa tree is no longer in the backyard,
the parrot left the front door, they weren't
middle class.
She was still spindly, she was still scared, she
still watched the woods not the news.

Why?

Because I like stupid tv shows.
Because food tastes better when the edges are charcoal and the center pudding.
Because tanbark on my feet is smoother than silk.
Because if I fixed the chair, it wouldn't squeak when I rock back and forth.
Because when the zipper comes loose and all my crap falls out it reminds me what's in there.
Because the bee stings are worth it.
Because when I show up late, I don't have time to be anxious.
Because there are no wrong steps when dancing alone.
Because it works just fine with a cracked screen.
Because mildew smells like home.
Because it adds character.
Because.

Life is too short to waste it on perfection.

Carrying a Parcel

I swim after the red eyes
   in the ever changing current.
We share a path

                 not a destination.

Baby birds, rowed and strangled in my
belly, chirp in fear at every jostle and
swerve.

I say to them,
          "Be silent little ones.
For your noise will cause me to err,
and if I err the red eyes will kill us.
Then no one would have the fortune
to drink from your nectar."

Tape Dispenser

Pop pop pop pop pop pop As the membrane
tears
Pale, plastic snail, Black shoe snail.
Gaping maul from which we grab
the tongue and pull, and pull, and pull
the smooth glossy film that
prays to go unseen. It is always seen.

Tiny sticky toddler hands
bend and pull the stick to stick
to stick to dirt and hair which pools
static underneath. So much hair,
poking out from festive wrappings,
peeling loose to catch a glimpse inside.

Pressed down perfectly pairing
patterns with memories in their
precious scrapbook. Pick, pick, pick,
pick of the nail at the edge
to pry the pasty plastic piece.
Screw this. I'll just use glue.

Welcome to the Big League

I come from a small pond
with small fish, a small world.
I thought myself as big
in this small pond where I curled.

The dam broke, where to go?
All these people who know
what they want, who they are.
I want to be heard.

Am I seen? Am I real?
A shadow passing surreal?
Am I fake? Am I gone?
Was I ever here for long?

All that skill and that flair
seems to have gone somewhere.
I'm lost in a sea of louder voices
screaming out their louder choices.

If somebody would notice me,

by some freak idiosyncrasy,
from small talk and chance meetings,
quick quips before seatings.

Would I cherish this friendly stalker?
I think not for, no one likes a gawker.
Perhaps this means that I ought,
become the seeker not the sought.

Where do you see yourself in five years?

I see myself walking
just walking, down a lane
a twisty curvy lane.
Not one that is a main
highway, or even well traveled.
I will hear
as I walk
the squirrels in the trees
and the cat
runs out of view
further
down the path.
I bring my camera up
too late to see.

Regret (and a bit of something else)

I follow pathed paths, each placed in winding ways,
none so direct as my aim was true those years past
when I would walk over trampled grass and low standing
walls that only ever barred me from my all important destination.

Today I count the bricks of the low standing wall, and make
note of the weeds growing out from its cracks. I never
stopped to care when I was a brick, purposeful and placed,
supporting and supported.

But now I have time to breath in the swaying branches
and follow the winding paths, so long as I watch out
for the weedkiller.

Parents Say

Parents say, as we all know,
"My teen years were the best!" and so,
they disregard your problems, fears.
"School is hard? Has you in tears?
Well maybe you just need to hear

of all those times I went through
all those years ago when I was young."
And they are hung, upon their own
feelings of those dreaded times.
Now as I write to you in rhymes
I say, don't follow similar crimes.

If a small one ever comes your way,
someone succumbs to the fray,
don't say life is easier, that life is like
a breezier holiday, just like a cruise
at your age. Say these are your views
on how they are spoiled, rotten, weak.
Instead give them the knowledge they seek:

That life was not easy way back when,
but it only gets harder with age. And then,
say that you'll be there to help them through.
Cause it only gets tougher, and you too

have been standing in their shoes
and know what it is like to lose.

And its okay, because life and strife,
go hand in hand like drum and fife.
So having one without the other,
is like a child without its mother.
And so, don't go with such dismay,
these somber words I don't mean to say,
but stay and hear me out I pray!

That when your mother or another
dismisses pain, give them a leg up.
Give them a clue, and they will do
the same for you.

Katie's New England Aesthetic

Sad houses,
tall houses with gingerbread,
repression,
drinking out of metal cups,
"Coming over to New England from England
and drinking out of weird metal cups."
The Scarlet Letter,
weird ominous events,
prisons that "have the stone gate and spikes",
oyster crackers.

In all fairness,
I am quite sure she has never been to New
England.
But we shan't ruin the surprise.

Ode to a Drunk Man

What dreadful wailing I do hear
coming from beneath my perch.
If I should but lend an ear
to the fool beneath this lovely birch.

I shall not complain that he did
interrupt my song with his.
But be it a waste, God forbid
I'll listen to what this poor man says

"O, for a draught of vintage! that hath been
cool'd a long age in the deep-delved earth,"
Enough draught has dribbled down your chin,
even insects would give you wide birth

"Away! away! for I will fly to thee,
Not charioted by Bacchus and his pards,"
Do not command the leave of me
shrill voice splinters into shards.

Why do you sing your noise so loud
then bid me fly away?
If you could not be so proud,
would not be better that I stay?

And so I shall, you foolish man.
My presence you should not fear.
So if you have no quarrels then
I think I'll stay right here.

"Thou wast not born for death, immortal Bird!
            No hungry generations tread thee
down;"
            Now what a quite preposterous word
            you said, which makes me frown.

            I'm honored that you think me such,
but mortal still I be.
Let me sing to you a touch
of hard cold reality.

See I shall die, much the same as you
and whether you see it plain,
my life is but an instant too
my struggles all in vain.

The Reunion: 20 Years of Friendship and Counting

Every time I see them
I notice they
are more like strangers
and less like me.

From Liala (Repair the Dam)

When did the slamming of doors and muffled
sobs echoing from the depths of this house
begin to feel like another leak
cracking through the dam wall?

And I, the dam keeper, whose wavering
vigilance
sets the whole valley below at risk, those
sprawling
houses and shops and parks and schools
blissfully
unaware of the building pressure. When did it
start?

That the bloody scissors found their way
into my hands, to be stashed out of sight and
mind?
The most garish of Easter Egg hunts that I
mustn't find any joy in, what a psychopath.

My number isn't magneted to anyone's fridge
last I checked, but the line's still hot.

No one has ever asked why I cling to my phone
so tightly, ever vigilant for the tiny blinking
light.

When did it start? That heads of house kept
bashing their's together, shaking the house
foundation.
And I, the offspring, wedged in between,
fingers and toes spread wide to hold back the
flood.

When did it start? Talking out of both mouths,
befriending axis and allies alike to urge peace.
Leaving I, the only enemy who talked behind
every back with half truths and deceit.

When did it start? That I began to know my tears
as the bandaids for others? My words as the
balm and scalpel alike, surgeons tools on the
battlefield?
And I, the liar, trusted by none, used by all.

From Justin (5 step plan)

5 stairs in the case, this five step plan
fanned out like the hand I was dealt,
full house, two parents, three kids,
just shy of a straight flush, no rush
to escape, got time, gotta plan. Step 1:

Learn lots, listen close every drop of
liquid knowledge, can't be parched in
the desert, 40 days or year, reap
that manna when it falls, we're drowning
out here, gotta learn it all. Step 2:

Grow strong, deep roots, tall stem,
leaf up and open so it won't be
shaken when the pot's repotted,
plotted down in a new plot, gotta
be sure my spine's built strong. Step 3:

Run far, by boat or car or sky,
rare dreams of focus I would fly
to new lands, new places, mapping

out new faces, taking in the mirror
of God's design. Step 4:

Build up, foundational, past
educational, hunting to gather those
good folk, hardy stock, architects
to fix society, turn ruins into scaffolds
of Babel 2.0. Step 5:

Collapse at last under the old
bent willow, to rest, for once
completely at ease. All's fixed
and right, gentle into that goodnight.

From Candace
(Endurance)

12 hour, physical labor, no breaks,
1 hour drive either way,
105° F, no breeze, no pay,
no problem. I can do that.

8 months, through winter, top bunk
next to the air conditioner,
messy floor, tense glares, no peace,
no problem. I can do that.

24 hrs, no food, no blanket,
9 miles, swarming bugs,
wet shoes, no map, no signal,
no problem. I can do that.

But for the love of God,
don't ask me to care.

From Bobby (Read Aloud)

Barbigerous
Uggle
Taradiddle

Wabbit
Hullaballoo
Alakazam
Teazel

Onomatopoeia
Febricula

Fipple
Unigravida
Nincompoop
?

From Alex (The Phoenix Waking)

Radial Array of rainbows fractured
like crystal against the wall, the covers,
A morning gift from the sun.
The chirp and mew of two shadowed forms
batting at belongings, creeping past my head,
scritch scratching on the door to be fed.

Numbing warmth of the covers, and the sun,
and my little shadows. I open my eyes
to see the contents of my mind splayed out
like a map of my soul, my room
the canvas, the nest, the fortress.
Thus wakes the hatchling of every new day.

The Taste of Childhood

Grains of sand brought to the lake side,
gritty grinding between crooked pearly whites,
lasted for days after.

My mom's chicken soup, best I ever had.
Just noodles, chicken, broth, a simple perfection
but shone like a whirlpool of the brightest citrine
gems.

Sweet watermelon, sticky red juices,
that dribbled down my chin with every bite,
slipping around dense black seeds. They mustn't
be swallowed.

My grandma's turkey burgers, made with her
own
folded hands. I smell them still whenever
the NFL tune plays over the tv.

The musty smell of books stacked close
in our old apartment. The air was damp and
mold

would grow in dappled spots along every
fore-edge.

A peanut butter bagel every morning's breakfast.
Warm and soft outside, crisp crunch in the
middle.
The bite of happiness to start each day.

The Holey Bucket

One day I told my parents
"I want to be an artist."
"Don't be an artist." Said my mother
Whose hands had taught me to carve truths in
charcoal
And shown me how to sculpt the heavens of my
brain into polymer clay.
"Artists don't make any money." She said "And
I don't
Want my little girl to marry a man she does not
love
Cause she cannot afford to feed herself."
And my father said "Do whatever makes you
happy!
I had hoped you would become an astronaut, but
I will love you anyway and keep you safe and
fed as long as I live."

One day, I was a child
Sitting in a small room with the other girls.
And while they painted their faces to attract a
mate,
I was painting my jeans, because the fabric was
such a good canvas
And I didn't need a mate, because I was an artist

God of my own creations, benevolent and cruel
and quiet and kind.
Making perfect things out of broken pieces
And blowing life into dead pigments.
Into queendoms, forests, people and creatures
who needed no one but me.
And my father said, how excited he was every
time
I started a new art piece. Cause he couldn't wait
to see what it would be.

One day, I was a teenager
Sitting with my friend who had been cut
on the jagged edges of this broken world.
And these paint covered hands couldn't clear
away
All the tears that threatened to drown us.
And I couldn't stop what was hurting him, I
couldn't fix
What was broken, but I could tell tell him a story
About himself, as I saw him.
And it gave him strength to make it through
another day,
Another week, another month, and then another
Until the wounds scabbed over, and he didn't
need an artist anymore.

One day, I was an adult
Living at home with my parents.

They loved me so I wasn't forced to stay in the
basement.
I listened in shame as they mentioned their
aching backs
Which housed me, their sore feet which brought
food to my plate.
And my father said, he couldn't do it anymore.
His eyes were too weak
To read the addresses, his legs too tired to walk
straight.
And my mother cried, because she had spent her
life teaching me,
And the state didn't like that, and she didn't
know if she could get
Her teaching license back and…
My brother cried, because he had been so
excited for college next year
But scholarships were hard to come by, and his
essays were not so good and…

One day I cried,
Because I was an artist.
And that meant I would never be able to repay
my parents
And return all the love they had poured into me.
Because these hands cannot turn rocks into
bread,
Or kind words into a warm coat,

Or turn the morning sunshine into a roof over
our heads.
If I had known, as I hurtled towards that cliff
with wings made of dreams
Believing I would soar instead of fall, would I
have been able to stop?